THE
DECEPTION
OF KATHRYN
VASK

Mark Steensland

BROADWAY PLAY PUBLISHING INC
New York
www.broadwayplaypublishing.com
info@broadwayplaypublishing.com

cover image design: Mark Steensland

First edition: April 2020
I S B N: 978-0-88145-874-9

Book design: Marie Donovan
Page make-up: Adobe InDesign
Typeface: Palatino

DEDICATION

To Ira Levin and Anthony Shaffer

ACKNOWLEDGEMENTS

Special thanks to John Lamb and Lyndsay Burch of the B Street Theatre in Sacramento, California, for staging the first public performance of this work in their New Play Brunch series.

CHARACTERS

KATHRYN VASK, *female. 36-years old. A woman in the grip of grief over the accidental death of her nine-year old son Timothy. She feels both responsible and guilty and is stuck in a state of utter loss. She has faith in God and believes in the supernatural.*

JONATHAN VASK, *male. 39-years old.* KATHRYN'*s husband. He is very frustrated about his wife's state of mind. He thinks she should have moved on by now and he is becoming desperate to find a way to make that happen. He is an atheist and has zero belief in anything supernatural.*

FATHER MICHAEL CADIGAN, *A K A* FATHER MIKE, *male. 29-years old. A Catholic priest who loves to wear his clerical clothing. He knows how* JONATHAN *feels about what he represents, but he also wants very much to help* KATHRYN.

LESLIE HARMON, *female. 59-years old. A psychic medium.*

ALBERT HARMON, *male. 63-years old.* LESLIE'*s husband and assistant.*

SETTING

The action takes place entirely in the main room of the VASK *home: an open floor plan which includes both the sitting and dining areas. A large dining table with six chairs occupies downstage right. Upstage right is a sideboard next to the door into the kitchen. Upstage left is a table with liquor bottles, a tray, glasses, and ice bucket. To the left of the liquor table is a fireplace. On the mantel are pictures of Timothy Vask at various ages. The largest shows Timothy at age nine. Downstage left is a short entryway that leads to the front door. Upstage center is a staircase with a landing halfway where the stairs have an L-bend. Downstage center is a couch, coffee table, chair, two end tables and lamps. Windows with opaque curtains occupy much of the wall space.*

EPIGRAPH

What a tangled web we weave when first we practice
to deceive.
Sir Walter Scott, *Marmion*

ACT ONE

Scene 1

(On rise, the entire stage is dark except for faint blue moonlight through the curtains.)

(JONATHAN VASK is in his pajamas on the couch, asleep under a blanket, snoring lightly until:)

(A blood-curdling scream shatters the silence.)

KATHRYN: *(O S)* Jonathan? Jonathan!

(JONATHAN switches the lamp on and squints against its brightness as he sits up.)

JONATHAN: I'm down here. In the living room.

(JONATHAN throws the blanket back and stands as KATHRYN VASK appears in a nightgown, rushing down the stairs and into his arms, sobbing.)

KATHRYN: Oh, Jonathan. It was terrible. And then you weren't there. I woke up and you weren't there.

JONATHAN: Sh-sh. I'm here now. Deep breaths. Come on. In. Out. In. Out.

(KATHRYN complies.)

JONATHAN: Better?

(KATHRYN nods against JONATHAN's chest, still holding him tightly.)

JONATHAN: Same one as last night?

KATHRYN: No. Worse. The worst one yet.

JONATHAN: How so?

(KATHRYN *shakes her head.*)

KATHRYN: Please…I don't want to talk about it.

(JONATHAN *leans back and lifts her chin, forcing her to make eye contact.*)

JONATHAN: But you have to, Kathryn.

KATHRYN: Doctor's orders?

JONATHAN: It is what he said.

(KATHRYN *pushes away from* JONATHAN.)

KATHRYN: I told you: I don't think he knows what he's doing.

(JONATHAN *drops onto the couch, exhausted.*)

JONATHAN: Not this again.

KATHRYN: Yes, this again.

JONATHAN: Doctor Tanner is one of the best in his field.

KATHRYN: I know. He's got a great big glass cabinet full of awards to prove it.

JONATHAN: Only you don't think they do.

KATHRYN: No, I don't. Not like that. It's just… I don't know. It's as if he thinks he's the best, too.

JONATHAN: Isn't he?

KATHRYN: You don't understand.

JONATHAN: I'm trying to.

KATHRYN: It's like he's frustrated that I'm not making progress.

JONATHAN: Aren't you?

KATHRYN: Of course. But he's angry about it. As if my not getting better is somehow making him look bad.

(JONATHAN *nods slowly.*)

KATHRYN: Understand now?

JONATHAN: Yes. But are you sure?

KATHRYN: You think I'm making it up?

JONATHAN: I didn't say that.

KATHRYN: You didn't have to.

(JONATHAN *props his elbows on his knees and holds his head in his hands.*)

JONATHAN: And that's exactly why I asked you the question. Because it's what you always do: assume what people are thinking and then hold them responsible for it, even if it's not true.

KATHRYN: What?

(JONATHAN *lifts his head.*)

JONATHAN: I know what I'm talking about. You do it to me all the time.

KATHRYN: When?

JONATHAN: Do we really need to relive Christmas again?

KATHRYN: Can't you let that go?

JONATHAN: I'd love to. Only you won't let me.

KATHRYN: You're the one who brought it up.

(JONATHAN *lifts his hands in surrender.*)

JONATHAN: Okay. Forget it. Let's just talk about Doctor Tanner.

KATHRYN: Yes. Let's.

JONATHAN: Did he tell you he was angry with you?

(KATHRYN *hesitates.*)

KATHRYN: Not in so many words.

(JONATHAN *raises his eyebrows.* KATHRYN *points her finger at him like a gun.*)

KATHRYN: Like that, though. Exactly like that.

JONATHAN: And what did my eyebrows say?

KATHRYN: That you don't believe me. That you think I'm a stupid bitch. That you're sorry you ever met me, let alone married me.

JONATHAN: You're right.

KATHRYN: What?

JONATHAN: Not about any of that. Just that yes, sometimes people say things without words. And despite all of his awards, Doctor Tanner is still a human being. Which means he has good days and bad days exactly like everyone else.

(KATHRYN *bites her cuticles as she considers this.*)

JONATHAN: So maybe he is a little frustrated with how slowly you're recovering. But maybe he also had bad sushi for lunch one day.

KATHRYN: I guess so.

JONATHAN: Want me to tell you what you're thinking all the time?

(KATHRYN *drops into the chair opposite the couch.*)

KATHRYN: No.

JONATHAN: Of course not.

KATHRYN: It's more than that, though. When I talk to him, I can tell he's not really listening.

JONATHAN: Because of his eyebrows?

KATHRYN: Two sessions ago, I told him about Timothy's dream of going to Venice. And when I brought it up again last time, he acted like it was the first I'd mentioned it.

(JONATHAN *knits his brows together and nods again.*)

KATHRYN: What are you thinking?

(JONATHAN *meets* KATHRYN'*s eyes and shrugs.*)

JONATHAN: Okay.

KATHRYN: Okay what?

JONATHAN: Maybe you shouldn't see him anymore.

KATHRYN: Really?

JONATHAN: If he's not helping.

(KATHRYN *joins* JONATHAN *on the couch and hugs him.*)

KATHRYN: Thank you.

JONATHAN: For what?

KATHRYN: For agreeing with me. It's exactly what I told him.

(JONATHAN *pulls away.*)

JONATHAN: You mean you already quit?

KATHRYN: I was going to tell you.

JONATHAN: When?

KATHRYN: I was waiting for a moment when you're not seething with rage. So never, I guess.

(JONATHAN *stands.*)

JONATHAN: Any wonder why I am?

KATHRYN: Being married to me has always been reason enough, hasn't it?

JONATHAN: I've never said that. And don't say "You didn't have to". It's not fair what you do. I give you the right to tell me how you feel. Is it my problem that you don't do it?

KATHRYN: Apparently.

JONATHAN: I love you, Kathryn. I'm sorry this is happening to us. I'm sorry about what happened to Timothy. But I'm tired of sleeping on the couch because I can't sleep in the same bed with you anymore. Not with all your tossing and turning. And mumbling. That's the worst part. Mumbling his name over and over again. And that's on the nights you don't wake up screaming. (*He lets this settle, then:*) You need to get serious about this.

KATHRYN: Don't you think I am?

JONATHAN: You quit going to the doctor.

KATHRYN: You just said I should.

JONATHAN: Because I know how you are once you get an idea in your head. Like a bear trap. What I think doesn't matter.

KATHRYN: But you know I want these nightmares to stop.

JONATHAN: I hope so. And so do I. Only they're not going to stop if you won't do something about them.

KATHRYN: That's what I've been doing.

JONATHAN: Then you need to try harder.

KATHRYN: Now you sound like Doctor Tanner.

(JONATHAN *blows air out his nose as he goes to the liquor table and pours three fingers of Scotch into a tumbler.*)

KATHRYN: Maybe I should just do what you do, huh? Paint everything over with a nice smooth coat of Scotch? For God's sake, Jonathan, it's four A M.

JONATHAN: And I was hoping to go back to bed. Unlike you, I have to be at work in a few hours. How is this any different from your sleeping pills?

KATHRYN: Mine come with a prescription.

JONATHAN: And a bigger bill. *(He drains the glass and slams it down.)*

KATHRYN: But we don't have to worry about that anymore, do we.

JONATHAN: No. We don't. Only for some reason, we still are.

KATHRYN: How can you say that?

JONATHAN: It's true, isn't it? On both counts.

KATHRYN: Because it's blood money.

JONATHAN: It's not. What happened to Timothy was an accident. That's what insurance is for.

KATHRYN: And would you be telling him the same thing if it was my policy you collected on?

JONATHAN: Don't make it sound so morbid.

KATHRYN: But it is.

JONATHAN: It wasn't when you wrecked your car in college.

KATHRYN: That's different.

JONATHAN: And your mother? She would have lost everything if your dad didn't have life insurance.

(KATHRYN turns away.)

KATHRYN: You know how I feel.

(JONATHAN goes back to the couch and kneels in front of KATHRYN. He puts his hands on her shoulders.)

JONATHAN: It wasn't your fault.

KATHRYN: It was.

JONATHAN: You weren't even here when it happened.

KATHRYN: Exactly.

(JONATHAN stands again.)

JONATHAN: So it's really my fault, then. That's what you're saying.

KATHRYN: No. What? How?

JONATHAN: I talked you into it, didn't I? I told you to hire Mrs Willingham so you could go back to work part time instead of being cooped up here all day waiting for Timothy to have another seizure.

KATHRYN: It wasn't like that.

JONATHAN: You say that now. Only I remember all the times I listened to you tell me how ashamed you were for feeling the way you did.

(KATHRYN *pushes tears off her cheeks.*)

KATHRYN: Stop it. Shut up.

JONATHAN: No. Doctor Tanner is right about one thing: this isn't going to get better if you won't talk about it. Our son is dead.

(KATHRYN *stands up fast, fists balled.*)

KATHRYN: I know!

JONATHAN: Nothing can change that.

KATHRYN: I know!

JONATHAN: And it's not. Your. Fault!

(KATHRYN *waits, debating internally for several seconds before speaking.*)

KATHRYN: But what if he thinks it is?

(*This brings everything to a full stop.* JONATHAN *stares.*)

JONATHAN: Doctor Tanner?

KATHRYN: No. Timothy. What if Timothy thinks it is my fault? What if he blames me for what happened?

JONATHAN: He can't blame you, Kathryn. He's dead.

KATHRYN: His body maybe. But not his spirit.

(JONATHAN *closes his eyes and lowers his head.*)

KATHRYN: Look, I'm sorry you don't believe what I do.

JONATHAN: I'm not.

KATHRYN: Well I am. It would make things easier if you did.

JONATHAN: The way it did with Bill and Janet?

KATHRYN: Why are bad examples the only examples for you?

JONATHAN: Bill and Janet are far from the only bad example.

KATHRYN: Going to tell me about your parents again? What a horrible person your dad was in spite of being a church elder.

JONATHAN: You say that as if it isn't true.

(KATHRYN *sarcastically feigns surprise.*)

KATHRYN: You're not telling me what I think, are you?

(JONATHAN *narrows his eyes.*)

JONATHAN: No. I'm commenting on your non-verbal communication.

KATHRYN: You're reading it wrong. I do think what you told me about your parents is true. But I also think you let it take the blame for a little too much.

JONATHAN: You're one to talk.

KATHRYN: What does that mean?

JONATHAN: We're not standing in the living room at four in the morning because of my problems.

KATHRYN: You've had thirty years to get over your shit. It's only been three months since Timothy died.

JONATHAN: And how much longer will you keep making black Xs on that grief calendar of yours?

KATHRYN: As long as it takes!

JONATHAN: See.

KATHRYN: See what?

JONATHAN: If you were serious about getting better, you wouldn't be so open-ended with it. *(He pours another drink.)*

KATHRYN: So I should set a date for when I'll be over the death of my son?

JONATHAN: Why not? That's the way most things are. Like those diets you're always on. Or school. Or work. Know how many deadlines I'm juggling right now?

KATHRYN: That's just like you. Treating this as if it's one of your construction jobs. Here's the blueprint. Here's the date we can open the road for traffic.

JONATHAN: And what's wrong with that?

KATHRYN: Because that's not the way hearts work. Brains, maybe. Not hearts.

JONATHAN: Not yours, you mean.

KATHRYN: Not yours, either. I know you try to cover it up a lot of the time. Like now. And it might fly at work where you can play the part of the 'tough boss' and they all believe you. But I know better. Your heart is one of the reasons I fell in love with you.

(JONATHAN sighs.)

JONATHAN: That was a long time ago.

KATHRYN: So?

JONATHAN: Things change. I know I have. And now this. It's changed us.

KATHRYN: For the worse?

JONATHAN: This isn't my idea of marital bliss.

KATHRYN: Then maybe stop trying to force us to fit whatever picture you've got in that brain of yours and let us be what we are instead.

JONATHAN: That's what you said about Timothy.

KATHRYN: What choice did we have? No one plans to have a child that isn't perfectly healthy. But we certainly couldn't blame him for it. We had to love him for who he was, problems and all. Shouldn't we feel the same way about each other?

(JONATHAN *looks at the glass in his hand.*)

JONATHAN: I don't want to end up like my parents.

(KATHRYN *takes the glass from him and sets it on the tray.*)

KATHRYN: Who would?

JONATHAN: You're right. I'm sorry. I just thought things would be different. That I'd feel the way I did after my father died.

KATHRYN: Relieved, you mean.

JONATHAN: That sounds so terrible when you say it out loud.

KATHRYN: It's okay. I understand. I've had the same sort of thoughts.

JONATHAN: You have?

KATHRYN: Of course. Taking care of Timothy wasn't easy. But I never wished he was… well… you know.

(JONATHAN *nods.*)

KATHRYN: Although Doctor Tanner said it's common for caregivers to feel that way. To want to be free of the responsibility. Permanently. And he kept trying to convince me that's what my problem is. That I feel guilty about wishing him gone and then having it happen. As if I somehow believe they're connected. Like my wish caused what happened.

JONATHAN: That makes sense.

KATHRYN: For some people maybe. But not for me. I know I didn't make it happen. My problem is I can't stop thinking about what was going through his head at the end. *(Her breath catches on a sob, but she pushes it down.)* I was always there for him. And then, when he needed me the most, I wasn't. And I'm so afraid that when he…passed out of this life, he felt betrayed and angry and he hated me for not being there.

(KATHRYN *breaks down.* JONATHAN *hugs her tightly.)*

JONATHAN: No. Deep breaths, now. Come on. In. Out. In. Out.

(KATHRYN *complies again, but it takes longer than before for her to calm down.)*

JONATHAN: You don't know that's what he felt.

KATHRYN: But I don't know that it isn't. And I can't stop thinking about it. The harder I try, the worse it gets.

JONATHAN: Like your nightmares.

KATHRYN: That's exactly what Doctor Tanner said. Apparently I'm going through an existential crisis. A "boundary situation" or something.

JONATHAN: What's that?

KATHRYN: When a person wants something they can't have.

JONATHAN: Because you want to stop thinking about Timothy, but you can't.

KATHRYN: No. Because I want to know that he forgives me. I have to know.

JONATHAN: But that's not possible.

KATHRYN: Isn't it?

(JONATHAN *stares at* KATHRYN.)

KATHRYN: Please don't look at me like that.

JONATHAN: You really think he's out there somewhere.

KATHRYN: Yes.

JONATHAN: Just because you believe something doesn't make it true.

KATHRYN: But your not believing makes it untrue?

JONATHAN: Okay. Stop. I think we've had this argument enough times to know what the outcome is going to be.

KATHRYN: So?

(JONATHAN *thinks a moment, then realizes:*)

JONATHAN: This is why you quit seeing Doctor Tanner.

KATHRYN: He doesn't believe me either.

JONATHAN: You thought he would?

KATHRYN: I didn't know. At least he had a more open mind about it than you.

JONATHAN: What?

KATHRYN: He said faith can be a powerful tool in recovery. If you believe something can make you better, then sometimes it does.

JONATHAN: So if you pray to be healed and you really believe it then you can be?

KATHRYN: Right.

JONATHAN: Bullshit. You can't cure cancer by asking your invisible friend to help you wish it away.

KATHRYN: I don't have cancer.

JONATHAN: I don't see the difference.

KATHRYN: I know you don't.

JONATHAN: Then what are you saying?

(KATHRYN *takes a moment to muster her strength.*)

KATHRYN: I want to see Father Mike.

(JONATHAN *smiles bitterly, without showing his teeth.*)

JONATHAN: And you were going to tell me about this, too, I suppose.

KATHRYN: Of course.

JONATHAN: Right after you told me about not seeing Doctor Tanner anymore.

KATHRYN: That was my plan.

JONATHAN: Why am I not surprised.

KATHRYN: Because you know me as well as I know you.

JONATHAN: I'm not sure about that.

KATHRYN: I wanted you to understand that I tried your way first. I really did.

JONATHAN: Did you?

KATHRYN: More than you've ever tried mine.

JONATHAN: For good reason.

KATHRYN: I could say the same thing.

JONATHAN: See? Like a bear trap.

KATHRYN: It could be worse, you know. I could be like your mother.

JONATHAN: That would be worse.

(JONATHAN *stares at the drink on the tray.* KATHRYN *takes his hands in her own.*)

KATHRYN: Forgive me?

JONATHAN: For what?

KATHRYN: All of this.

JONATHAN: You know I do.

KATHRYN: It would be nice to hear it.

JONATHAN: I forgive you.

KATHRYN: And do you still love me?

JONATHAN: I do.

(JONATHAN *and* KATHRYN *hug gently.*)

KATHRYN: Ready to go back to bed?

(JONATHAN *nods and heads for the couch.*)

KATHRYN: You can go upstairs if you want. I'm staying up. Maybe try and sleep later.

JONATHAN: Thanks.

(JONATHAN *takes his pillow and blanket with him upstairs.*)

JONATHAN: Wake me if I'm not up by seven.

KATHRYN: Okay. Good night.

JONATHAN: Night.

(KATHRYN *waits until* JONATHAN*'s gone, then crosses the room to the sideboard by the dining table.*)

(*She opens the center door and reaches behind a stack of plates to take out a Rubik's Cube. She stares at it.*)

(*After a beat, she looks over her shoulder, as if she expects to see Timothy standing in the corner. But there's no one there.*)

KATHRYN: (*Whispering*) Timothy? (*She listens to the clock ticking for a few moments, then puts the Rubik's Cube back in the sideboard and goes through the swinging door into the kitchen.*)

(*From somewhere, a breeze moves the curtains.*)

(*Black out*)

Scene 2

(Afternoon sunlight shines through the opaque curtains.)

(Rolls of blueprints and a hard hat are on the dining table.)

(An overstuffed leather briefcase is on one of the chairs; a suit coat hangs on the back of another.)

(JONATHAN enters through the swinging door from the kitchen, carrying a plate loaded with cheese and crackers.)

(He sets the plate next to the hard hat, then loosens his tie and walks to the table to pour two fingers of Scotch into a glass.)

(The doorbell rings. Irritated, Jonathan checks his watch, then quickly drinks the Scotch and sets the glass back down.)

(He goes to the front door and opens it, revealing FATHER MICHAEL CADIGAN standing outside. He's dressed in clerical clothing: black shoes, black pants, a short sleeve black shirt and a white tab collar. Jonathan is not pleased to see him.)

FATHER MIKE: Hello, Jonathan.

JONATHAN: You said on the phone this wouldn't take long.

FATHER MIKE: I hope not.

JONATHAN: Makes two of us. Come in then. Let's get it over with.

(JONATHAN returns to the table in the corner and pours another two fingers of Scotch.)

(FATHER MIKE wipes his feet on the mat outside, then steps in and closes the door.)

JONATHAN: I hope this isn't some kind of trick.

FATHER MIKE: Excuse me?

JONATHAN: Another something you and Kathryn have cooked up to try and save my soul. Like that charity golf tournament two summers ago.

FATHER MIKE: *(Smiling)* No. Not exactly.

JONATHAN: Good. Because what I told you about how I feel still stands.

FATHER MIKE: I'm sure it does.

(JONATHAN *picks up the glass of Scotch.)*

JONATHAN: Still not drinking or can I pour you one?

FATHER MIKE: No, thank you.

(JONATHAN *makes a "cheers" gesture and takes a sip.)*

JONATHAN: So what's this all about?

FATHER MIKE: Kathryn came to see me today.

JONATHAN: Against my wishes.

FATHER MIKE: I know.

JONATHAN: Which reminds me. I've been wondering about that. Should she?

FATHER MIKE: I don't follow.

JONATHAN: Should she be going against my wishes. What I mean to say is: didn't she promise to obey me at our wedding? In sickness and in health. Until death do us part. Aren't I the head of the house according to you?

FATHER MIKE: That's a rather complicated issue.

(JONATHAN *laughs.* FATHER MIKE *stares at him, distressed.)*

FATHER MIKE: What's so funny?

JONATHAN: It's a great opening line. Really sets the stage, doesn't it? *(He takes another sip of Scotch.)* Because if you say something is complicated right off the bat, you put yourself in the position of power, don't you.

Come to think of it, I do the same thing all the time. At work. In meetings with clients. I always start off by saying something like: "This is going to be the biggest, hardest job we've ever done". Even if it isn't. Especially if it isn't. Then they're amazed when we finish ahead of schedule and under budget.

(FATHER MIKE *checks his watch.*)

JONATHAN: There's a switch. Shouldn't it be me checking my watch while you're talking?

FATHER MIKE: Sorry, it's just that I don't think we have much time before Kathryn gets home.

JONATHAN: Right. Right. Sorry. Carry on then. Let's talk about Kathryn. I assume that during her visit she told you what's been going on since the funeral?

FATHER MIKE: Yes.

JONATHAN: The nightmares?

FATHER MIKE: Yes.

JONATHAN: Did she describe them to you?

FATHER MIKE: Yes.

JONATHAN: In detail?

FATHER MIKE: Seemed like it.

JONATHAN: Did she tell you the one where she drowns in her own tears?

(FATHER MIKE *nods.*)

JONATHAN: Did she also tell you that I arranged— and paid—for her to see the best, most expensive psychiatrist in the entire state.

FATHER MIKE: I saw him on Oprah once.

JONATHAN: She stopped seeing him because she decided he didn't know what he was talking about. You, on the other hand, do.

(FATHER MIKE *sighs.*)

FATHER MIKE: I understand how you feel about this. Really.

JONATHAN: No. I don't think you do. I don't think you can. And that's another thing that's always bothered me about you blackshirts. You don't get married yourself, but then you have the balls to talk to me about what it's like to be married. You don't have children, but you think you have some idea of what it's like to lose a child.

FATHER MIKE: That's not what I meant.

JONATHAN: What did you mean then?

FATHER MIKE: You're angry.

JONATHAN: Shouldn't I be?

FATHER MIKE: That's the part I understand. And I know you may not believe me but I'm here to help you.

JONATHAN: Is that what Kathryn said? That I'm the one who needs help?

FATHER MIKE: Can you shut up and listen to me for one minute!

(FATHER MIKE'*s outburst shocks* JONATHAN *into silence.*)

FATHER MIKE: Kathryn told me that she wants to know Timothy forgives her for what happened.

JONATHAN: Might as well be the moon, huh?

(FATHER MIKE *gives* JONATHAN *a withering look.*)

JONATHAN: Right. Sorry.

(JONATHAN *mimes locking his lips and throwing away the key.*)

FATHER MIKE: I told her Timothy's death was an accident. A tragic accident. But an accident all the same. Because of that, she has no reason to even think that he would blame her. But she said my word wasn't enough. And then she asked me what I knew about contacting him.

(JONATHAN *stands up straighter.*)

JONATHAN: Timothy?

FATHER MIKE: That's right.

JONATHAN: Like how? Like a…what are they called?

FATHER MIKE: A séance.

JONATHAN: That's it. Is that what she meant?

FATHER MIKE: Yes. Under any other circumstances, I would have immediately told her to stay as far away from those kinds of things as possible.

JONATHAN: Really?

FATHER MIKE: Oh, yes. Such activity is strictly forbidden.

JONATHAN: I thought you'd like that sort of thing. Prove to the skeptics that there's life after death.

FATHER MIKE: On the contrary. Spiritualism is very dangerous.

JONATHAN: Because of what? Fraud?

(FATHER MIKE *shakes his head.*)

FATHER MIKE: I know you don't believe anything I'm about to tell you, but I'll say it anyway so you can understand my position. Hopefully.

JONATHAN: Go on.

FATHER MIKE: When someone dies, they don't go to heaven immediately.

JONATHAN: That's not what my father told me. After my grandmother passed, he used to say she was watching me all the time to make sure I was being a good boy.

FATHER MIKE: I'm sorry for that. It's a common misconception.

JONATHAN: A different version of the same lie, you mean.

FATHER MIKE: If you insist. My point is that the dead are not in heaven. Not yet. They are sleeping.

JONATHAN: Sleeping? Now there's something I can look forward to. *(He makes a "cheers" gesture again and takes another sip.)*

FATHER MIKE: Until God wakes them up for the final judgement.

JONATHAN: Oh, I see. Always something, isn't there? And so it's dangerous because they'll be pissed off if you wake them up early?

FATHER MIKE: No. It's dangerous because you'll get a demon instead.

(JONATHAN can barely contain his laughter.)

JONATHAN: A demon?

FATHER MIKE: That's right. A demon who will masquerade as the dead person you are trying to contact.

JONATHAN: And then what will this demon do? Give you lousy advice about the stock market?

(JONATHAN laughs again as he finishes his drink and sets the empty glass down. FATHER MIKE sighs.)

FATHER MIKE: Why not?

JONATHAN: Are you serious?

FATHER MIKE: The devil approves of anything that brings you to ruin.

JONATHAN: Oh. So now we're talking about the devil.

FATHER MIKE: Yes.

JONATHAN: Horns? Cloven hooves? Spiked tail? Pitchfork? That guy?

FATHER MIKE: Another common misconception.

JONATHAN: Of course. And what did Kathryn have to say about all this?

FATHER MIKE: I didn't tell her.

JONATHAN: Aren't you supposed to be the good shepherd? And isn't she one of your sheep? Shouldn't you be protecting her from dangers like this?

FATHER MIKE: That's why I'm here.

JONATHAN: You want me to talk her out of it.

FATHER MIKE: No. I want you to help her.

JONATHAN: How?

FATHER MIKE: Hold a séance.

JONATHAN: You want me to help my wife try to contact my dead son?

FATHER MIKE: Yes.

JONATHAN: But aren't you afraid we'll get a demon?

FATHER MIKE: No. Because the séance won't be real.

JONATHAN: What's the point, then?

FATHER MIKE: There's an older couple I know from my college days. Albert and Leslie Harmon. They're actors. Early in their career, they were part of a spirit magic show.

JONATHAN: What's that?

FATHER MIKE: Like a séance, but played for fun. Where everyone knows it's not real. So they have some experience with this sort of thing. We tell Kathryn that they are for real. Then we hold the séance. They convince her that they've contacted Timothy and when she asks for his forgiveness—

(JONATHAN *suddenly understands.*)

JONATHAN: He gives it to her.

FATHER MIKE: Exactly.

JONATHAN: And she's cured.

FATHER MIKE: Hopefully.

(JONATHAN *slaps* FATHER MIKE *on the shoulder.*)

JONATHAN: I hate to admit it, but that's a very good idea.

FATHER MIKE: Given the situation, I thought so, too.

JONATHAN: You didn't tell her about any of this other stuff? About the demons and so on?

FATHER MIKE: Of course not. I suggested it to her, in fact.

JONATHAN: You told her she should have a séance?

FATHER MIKE: Not at first. I listened carefully to what she was saying. And I could tell from the way she talked about her need for Timothy's forgiveness that things would only get worse if something radical wasn't done.

JONATHAN: You're preaching to the choir.

FATHER MIKE: And I was about to tell her that she absolutely should not try to contact Timothy when I remembered the Harmons and it was like the whole idea popped into my head fully formed.

JONATHAN: What was her reaction?

FATHER MIKE: Can't you imagine? She was excited and relieved. When she left my office, she said she was going straight to the library to find out everything she could about doing one on her own. Which is why it's imperative that we act as quickly as possible.

JONATHAN: What do you want from me?

FATHER MIKE: Your support.

JONATHAN: But she knows I don't believe any of this bullshit. Pardon my French.

FATHER MIKE: You'll change your mind.

JONATHAN: No, I won't.

FATHER MIKE: I don't mean for real.

JONATHAN: You want me to pretend I've changed my mind.

FATHER MIKE: Right. And be convincing. If she feels you're in this with her, I think her recovery will be much, much stronger.

JONATHAN: Again, I hate to admit it, but I think you're right.

FATHER MIKE: You should take the same approach you did with that doctor. Insist that she has the absolute best in the field and then tell her that's who the Harmons are.

JONATHAN: Have you talked to them already?

FATHER MIKE: Right after Kathryn left and before I called you. They were quite excited about it.

JONATHAN: How much will this cost me?

FATHER MIKE: Not as much as that doctor.

JONATHAN: I hope not.

FATHER MIKE: Should I tell them you want to go through with it?

JONATHAN: Depends on Kathryn at this point. But yes.

FATHER MIKE: Good. Like I said, the sooner we can make this happen, the better.

(JONATHAN *gets a faraway look in his eyes.*)

JONATHAN: This must be what he meant.

FATHER MIKE: Who?

JONATHAN: Doctor Tanner. Kathryn told me that he said faith can be an important tool in recovery.

FATHER MIKE: You know I agree with that.

JONATHAN: He wasn't referring to God, though. More like if a person believes something can make them well—even when it can't—then it still might.

FATHER MIKE: The placebo effect.

JONATHAN: Right. I told her I thought it was nonsense. I said something like 'You can't wish cancer away.' Only now I see what he was talking about. Which means the more Kathryn believes the séance is for real—

FATHER MIKE: —the better her chance of getting past all this.

JONATHAN: Well, then: these actor friends of yours had better be the best.

FATHER MIKE: Rest assured. They are. I saw the show they were in. I was terrified.

JONATHAN: We're not trying to scare her.

FATHER MIKE: No. But a bit of fear will be helpful in this case, I think. To give some gravity to the events. We are dealing with ghosts, after all.

(JONATHAN *nods in agreement just as the front door opens and* KATHRYN *enters, a stack of library books in each arm.*)

KATHRYN: Jonath—? (*She stops short when she sees* FATHER MIKE.) What are you doing here?

JONATHAN: Telling me about your meeting.

KATHRYN: Oh.

(JONATHAN *steps toward* KATHRYN.)

JONATHAN: Let me help you with those.

KATHRYN: It's okay. I can manage. *(She tries to close the front door with her foot and the books slip from her grip and tumble to the floor.)*

*(*KATHRYN *drops to all fours to scoop them up. Jonathan kneels next to her.)*

JONATHAN: Don't worry. Father Mike told me everything already.

*(*JONATHAN *picks up one of the books,* Hearing the Dead *by Susan Straker, and hands it to* KATHRYN *gently.)*

KATHRYN: Really?

*(*JONATHAN *nods and picks up one of the stacks.* KATHRYN *picks up the other. They both stand.)*

KATHRYN: So how angry are you?

FATHER MIKE: Kathryn. Remember what we said about jumping to conclusions? Let him tell you how he feels first.

JONATHAN: You told her that?

KATHRYN: Yes, he did. And he's right. I'm sorry. Go ahead.

JONATHAN: I'm not mad.

KATHRYN: You're not?

JONATHAN: No.

KATHRYN: But you should be.

JONATHAN: I'm as surprised as you are.

*(*KATHRYN *stares, unsure.)*

KATHRYN: You're not kidding.

JONATHAN: No. I'm not.

FATHER MIKE: He isn't.

KATHRYN: And you're okay with it?

FATHER MIKE: He's getting there, Kathryn. Give him some time.

KATHRYN: But how can you be? You don't even believe it's possible.

JONATHAN: It has more to do with me wanting what you want.

KATHRYN: Really?

JONATHAN: You're telling me this is what you think will really help you. How can I say no to that?

KATHRYN: Oh, Jonathan.

(KATHRYN *throws the books on the couch and hugs* JONATHAN. *He struggles with the stack he's holding until* FATHER MIKE *steps forward and takes it.*)

JONATHAN: Father Mike deserves more credit than I do.

FATHER MIKE: I think we'll all be happy when Kathryn feels this thing is resolved.

(KATHRYN *drops her arms and steps back.*)

KATHRYN: I will.

FATHER MIKE: Well, then…if you'll excuse me.

KATHRYN: Won't you stay for dinner?

(FATHER MIKE *glances briefly at* JONATHAN, *then smiles.*)

FATHER MIKE: That's kind of you, but my dietary requirements are quite restrictive at the moment, I'm afraid.

KATHRYN: Some other time.

FATHER MIKE: After all this is over.

(KATHRYN *hugs* FATHER MIKE.)

KATHRYN: Thank you. For everything.

FATHER MIKE: Just doing my job.

JONATHAN: And doing it well, if you don't mind my saying so.

(KATHRYN *can hardly believe her ears.* JONATHAN *shakes hands with* FATHER MIKE.)

FATHER MIKE: That means a lot coming from you. Good night.

(KATHRYN *and* JONATHAN *wave. As soon as* FATHER MIKE *is through the door,* KATHRYN *faces* JONATHAN.)

KATHRYN: Do you really mean it? You're not angry? You want to help?

JONATHAN: Yes.

KATHRYN: Oh, Jonathan... I don't know what to say.

JONATHAN: Thank you?

KATHRYN: Of course thank you.

JONATHAN: You're welcome. And first thing tomorrow, I'll see what I can find out about who does this sort of thing. Hopefully there's someone local. I want to make sure we don't get a faker in it for the money. Only the best for you. Deal?

(KATHRYN *nods and hugs him tightly.* JONATHAN *looks over her shoulder at the books on the couch.*)

(*Black out*)

Scene 3

(*A week later. Pale moonlight shines through the opaque curtains on the windows.*)

(JONATHAN *paces back and forth center stage. The doorbell rings.*)

KATHRYN: (*O S*) Oh, no. They're early.

(JONATHAN *checks his watch.*)

JONATHAN: *(Quietly)* No, you're late. *(Calling upstairs)* It's okay. Take your time.

(JONATHAN *opens the front door.* FATHER MIKE *enters, alone.)*

FATHER MIKE: Are they here yet?

JONATHAN: No. I thought you were them.

(JONATHAN *closes the door.* FATHER MIKE *looks around the room.)*

FATHER MIKE: Where's Kathryn?

JONATHAN: Upstairs. Getting ready.

FATHER MIKE: How's she doing?

JONATHAN: Climbing the walls already. I wish we could just do the damn thing tonight and get it over with.

FATHER MIKE: What? No. Having this preliminary meeting was a brilliant idea.

JONATHAN: I hope so.

FATHER MIKE: Absolutely. Gives us the chance to set the stage, right? Like what you do at work with those clients of yours. Now don't forget: when they arrive, introduce me to them as if we've never met.

JONATHAN: I know. And keep your voice down. You'll derail the whole thing before we even get up to speed.

FATHER MIKE: The Harmons told me some of the things you worked out. I came up with a few bits myself. A research project they're part of.

JONATHAN: Good. You look like you could use a drink. Sure you don't want one?

FATHER MIKE: Heaven's no. That's the last thing I need in this situation. And you shouldn't either.

JONATHAN: Too late.

FATHER MIKE: Then don't have another. It loosens your tongue too much.

(JONATHAN's *comeback is preempted by the doorbell.*)

KATHRYN: *(O S)* Haven't you answered the door?

FATHER MIKE: He did. The first time was me.

KATHRYN: *(O S)* Oh, hello Father Mike.

FATHER MIKE: Hello, dear.

KATHRYN: *(O S)* I'll be down in a minute.

FATHER MIKE: Take your time.

(JONATHAN *opens the front door.*)

JONATHAN: Hello. Come in, please.

(ALBERT HARMON *enters first. He's a compact man with an intense jaw and eyes to match, wearing a dark gray suit over an open-collared black dress shirt.*)

(*He holds his hand out. His smile looks more like a grimace.*)

ALBERT: Albert Harmon.

(JONATHAN *shakes his hand.*)

JONATHAN: Nice to meet you in person. I'm Jonathan Vask.

ALBERT: My wife, Leslie.

(LESLIE HARMON *enters next. Her blonde hair is pulled back in a bun that tightens her sharp features. She wears a long black skirt and a black turtleneck with a purple crystal on a silver chain.*)

(JONATHAN *takes her hand.*)

JONATHAN: Thank you for doing this.

LESLIE: I'm always happy to help people with my gift.

JONATHAN: *(Loudly)* This is Father Michael Cadigan.

FATHER MIKE: *(Loudly)* Hello. Very nice to meet you.

(FATHER MIKE *shakes hands with both* ALBERT *and* LESLIE.)

ALBERT: Likewise.

(KATHRYN *reaches the landing and pauses when she sees* LESLIE *moving toward the pictures of Timothy on the mantel.*)

(KATHRYN *watches her for a beat, then noisily comes the rest of the way down the stairs.*)

KATHRYN: Sorry about that. Here I am.

(*Everyone faces* KATHRYN *at once and she freezes, as if caught in the act of doing something bad.*)

JONATHAN: It's all right, honey. Let me introduce you to the Harmons.

(KATHRYN *joins* JONATHAN.)

JONATHAN: This is Albert.

KATHRYN: Pleased to meet you.

(ALBERT *and* KATHRYN *shake hands.*)

JONATHAN: And this is his wife, Leslie.

(LESLIE *turns from the pictures.*)

LESLIE: Hello.

KATHRYN: I've never met a medium before. Is that what I should call you?

ALBERT: She prefers if you think of her as a guide.

KATHRYN: Oh?

LESLIE: Because I help people find each other. The sitting will create a thin place where the land of the living and the land of the dead can overlap enough for us to meet halfway, so to speak.

(KATHRYN *is enthralled.* JONATHAN *glances at* FATHER MIKE *and lifts his eyebrows: "She is good".*)

FATHER MIKE: I was telling Jonathan before you two arrived how glad I am that we're finally meeting.

ALBERT: Is that so?

FATHER MIKE: I've heard so much about you over the years.

ALBERT: All good, I hope.

FATHER MIKE: Unlike some others. I imagine you find it frustrating that there are so many frauds in your line of work.

JONATHAN: Something you have in common with them, right Father Mike?

FATHER MIKE: What?

KATHRYN: Jonathan!

JONATHAN: It's true. Seems like half the channels on T V are full of fakes begging for money on God's behalf.

FATHER MIKE: Fair enough.

KATHRYN: Don't encourage him. We'll be here all night.

JONATHAN: Sorry. Let me trade my soapbox for a glass of Scotch.

(FATHER MIKE *looks at* LESLIE.)

JONATHAN: Can I get anyone else a drink?

LESLIE: No.

JONATHAN: Albert?

ALBERT: She meant no for everyone.

(JONATHAN *stops and turns around.*)

JONATHAN: Excuse me?

LESLIE: You mustn't drink.

JONATHAN: But I already have been.

LESLIE: That's unfortunate. *(To* ALBERT*)* Didn't you tell him not to?

ALBERT: *(To* LESLIE*)* It's not a problem for tonight. *(To* JONATHAN*)* When we hold the sitting, however, it's very important that everyone is as clear-headed as possible.

JONATHAN: Okay.

*(*JONATHAN *glances at* FATHER MIKE *as he rejoins the group.)*

ALBERT: Are any of you on medication?

JONATHAN: Kathryn is. Sleeping pills.

KATHRYN: Only when I can't sleep.

*(*LESLIE *steps toward her, looking around her head, above it and to the sides.)*

LESLIE: That's not all, though.

*(*KATHRYN'*s eyes widen.* JONATHAN *looks at her.)*

JONATHAN: Isn't it?

KATHRYN: Something else Doctor Tanner gave me. To deal with my anxiety. *(To* LESLIE*)* How did you know?

LESLIE: They're in your aura like mud in a glass of water. Understand?

*(*KATHRYN *nods.)*

ALBERT: Don't get her wrong. She's not saying you shouldn't take them. Especially if the doctor has prescribed it for you. Just not when we're working.

KATHRYN: All right.

*(*KATHRYN *sees* JONATHAN *frowning. This makes her smile.)*

KATHRYN: Isn't that amazing? How she knew about the other medication.

JONATHAN: Remarkable.

ALBERT: May we sit down?

JONATHAN: Sorry. Please do.

(ALBERT *and* LESLIE *sit on the couch.* KATHRYN *sits in the chair opposite.* FATHER MIKE *and* JONATHAN *bring over chairs from the dining table.*)

ALBERT: Your husband gave us the basics of the situation on the phone. But Leslie would like to hear your version as well.

KATHRYN: All right. Where should I start?

ALBERT: Wherever you think.

(KATHRYN *takes a deep breath. She smiles at* JONATHAN, *then faces* LESLIE.)

KATHRYN: We met in college.

JONATHAN: I don't think he meant that far back.

ALBERT: Please, Mr Vask. What Leslie is doing now is like your blueprints over there. She needs to have a complete understanding of your wife's emotional energy so that she can construct the sitting in the most effective way possible. You wouldn't start building with a missing page, would you?

(JONATHAN *shakes his head.*)

JONATHAN: No. Sorry. Go ahead.

(KATHRYN's *smile becomes forlorn. She knows it's tough for* JONATHAN *and she really appreciates what he's doing.*)

LESLIE: You met in college.

KATHRYN: I was an art student. He was working on his Master's in civil engineering. We got married after I graduated. I found a good job at a small graphic design firm. But then Jonathan got this job and even though it was far from home for both of us, it was too good to pass up. So he accepted and we moved here. In a city this big, the competition in my field was off the

charts. I couldn't find full time work, so I freelanced
and taught elementary school art part time. Which was
fine because Jonathan was making more than enough
money. Starting a family seemed like the natural next
step. We had Timothy. Everything was great at first.
Until he had his first seizure when he was six months
old. I was still taking time off work and it became clear
pretty fast that I wouldn't be going back. The doctors
told us his epilepsy would be treatable, but after a few
years, they found out he was an unusual case. There
were a bunch of other complications and he wasn't
responding to the usual treatments. Sometimes he
would have seizures one after the other. I would have
to give him a special emergency medication to stop
them.

LESLIE: I'm sorry. That sounds like it was incredibly
difficult for you.

KATHRYN: And for Jonathan.

JONATHAN: Because it was hard on her.

LESLIE: Of course.

KATHRYN: It wasn't all bad.

LESLIE: I understand.

JONATHAN: But I saw it was taking a toll on her.
Mentally. Physically. And emotionally.

KATHRYN: Around when Timothy turned nine,
Jonathan said we should hire someone to come in so
that I could go back to work. Part time to start. Not for
the money, but to get out with other people my age.

LESLIE: Sounds like that was a good idea.

KATHRYN: Except it wasn't.

(KATHRYN's *tone sucks the air out of the room.*)

JONATHAN: Kathryn, honey: don't get mad at them.

LESLIE: Please, Mr Vask. Let her say what she wants. How she wants.

(KATHRYN *wavers between tears and rage.* LESLIE *leans forward.*)

LESLIE: It's okay. Keep going. Why wasn't it a good idea.

KATHRYN: Because it wouldn't have happened if I had been here. And Timothy knows that. And he blames me for it.

LESLIE: You seem certain.

KATHRYN: He's told me so. In some of my nightmares.

JONATHAN: What?

KATHRYN: That's why I didn't want to talk about them.

LESLIE: But that's not the only reason.

KATHRYN: No. I've…felt him, too.

LESLIE: When you were awake, you mean.

(KATHRYN *looks at* JONATHAN, *hesitating.*)

JONATHAN: Have you?

(KATHRYN *nods, then faces* LESLIE.)

KATHRYN: It's not like I've seen him or anything. It's been more a kind of pressure, I guess you could say.

LESLIE: A change in the atmosphere?

KATHRYN: Right. But negative, you know?

LESLIE: Heavy.

KATHRYN: That's a good word for it.

(LESLIE *closes her eyes and moves her head, as if listening to something in the distance.*)

LESLIE: It happened here, didn't it? In this room. (*She opens her eyes.*)

KATHRYN: Mrs Willingham found him at the bottom of the stairs.

ALBERT: She was the caregiver you hired?

(KATHRYN *nods.*)

KATHRYN: We think he had a seizure on the landing and then he fell down. Mrs Willingham was in the laundry room, so she didn't hear anything. By the time she found him, he was already…

(KATHRYN *closes her eyes tightly.* JONATHAN *takes her hand.*)

(LESLIE *stands. She holds the purple crystal in her left hand as she walks around the room.*)

(FATHER MIKE, JONATHAN, *and* KATHRYN *trade glances with each other while they wait.*)

LESLIE: I want to have the sitting in here. You'll need to move the furniture out of the way.

JONATHAN: Even the table?

ALBERT: We'll bring our own.

JONATHAN: What about the chairs?

ALBERT: Those will be fine. We'll record the sitting as well. Both audio and video.

FATHER MIKE: That's for the university, right?

(ALBERT *nods.*)

KATHRYN: University?

FATHER MIKE: Research project. The physics department at Kneale is studying paranormal phenomenon. Leslie is their main subject.

(KATHRYN *is even more impressed.*)

KATHRYN: Really?

ALBERT: That okay with you? The recording?

KATHRYN: Sure. Honey?

JONATHAN: That's fine.

ALBERT: Excellent. Thank you.

LESLIE: Did your husband tell you I need something that belonged to Timothy? For a focus object.

KATHRYN: The more personal, the better, right?

LESLIE: That's right.

(KATHRYN *stands and crosses the room to the sideboard near the dining table. She opens the center door and reaches behind the stack of plates to retrieve the Rubik's Cube.*)

(LESLIE *smiles when she sees it.* JONATHAN *doesn't.*)

LESLIE: Oh my goodness. I haven't seen one of those in years.

(JONATHAN *stands.*)

JONATHAN: I thought you got rid of that when Doctor Tanner told you to.

KATHRYN: I couldn't.

JONATHAN: No wonder he was no help. You wouldn't even do what he said.

KATHRYN: I did. Most of it. Just not this. (*To* LESLIE) It was Timothy's favorite. He had it with him when he died.

(LESLIE *nods slowly.*)

KATHRYN: That makes it better, right? One of the books I was reading said so.

LESLIE: Sounds like Susan Straker.

KATHRYN: It was. 'Hearing the Dead.'

LESLIE: Her best, in my opinion.

KATHRYN: So I was right? This is good?

LESLIE: It's perfect.

(KATHRYN *looks at* JONATHAN.)

KATHRYN: Then I'm glad I didn't get rid of it.

LESLIE: And I can take it with me? Until Friday?

KATHRYN: Promise to be careful with it?

LESLIE: Of course, dear. But if my taking it makes you uncomfortable.

KATHRYN: No, I'm sorry. I know you will. You must deal with this sort of thing all the time.

ALBERT: We do.

(KATHRYN *holds the Rubik's Cube out.* ALBERT *takes it from her and puts it into* LESLIE's *purse.*)

ALBERT: I think that about does it. Unless any of you have more questions...

(JONATHAN *and* KATHRYN *trade glances, then shake their heads.*)

ALBERT: Until Friday night, then.

(*Everyone ad-libs good-byes as* JONATHAN *and* KATHRYN *escort* ALBERT *and* LESLIE *out the door with* FATHER MIKE. *Once everyone is gone,* JONATHAN *heads straight to the liquor table.* KATHRYN *watches him grimly as he pours four fingers of Scotch into a glass.*)

KATHRYN: Aren't you going to tell me how mad you are?

JONATHAN: No. I want this to work and my getting mad won't help, will it?

(KATHRYN *shakes her head.*)

JONATHAN: Well, then. Cheers.

(JONATHAN *drinks his Scotch and goes upstairs.* KATHRYN *watches him for a long moment, then walks to the mantel and stares at Timothy's pictures. (Black out)*

END OF ACT ONE

ACT TWO

(The windows and doors have been covered with blackout drapes. The furniture has been moved out of the way, clearing the space where the couch was. In its place is a rack of lights between two cameras on tripods.)

(LESLIE is crouched next to a low table containing several other pieces of electronic gear. She searches through a metal box while KATHRYN watches.)

KATHRYN: Are you sure you'll be able to reach him?

LESLIE: I am. But it's important that you are, too.

KATHRYN: How long does it usually take?

LESLIE: The shortest sitting I've had lasted fifteen minutes. The longest was almost three hours.

KATHRYN: What happens first?

LESLIE: Alignment.

(Through the open front door, ALBERT and JONATHAN carry a five-sided pedestal table, its top covered with shapes and markings in various colors.)

ALBERT: Where do you want it?

LESLIE: Doesn't matter, until I get a reading. Do you know where the compass is?

(ALBERT and JONATHAN set the table down.)

ALBERT: Should be in the briefcase. The black leather one.

(LESLIE *stands.*)

LESLIE: And do you know where that is?

(FATHER MIKE *enters. When* ALBERT *sees he is carrying the black leather bag, he smiles.*)

ALBERT: Speak of the devil.

(FATHER MIKE *stops short.*)

FATHER MIKE: Excuse me?

(ALBERT *takes the bag from him.*)

ALBERT: An old expression. Comes from the belief that all it took to summon the devil was saying his name.

FATHER MIKE: I know that, but what does it have to do with me?

LESLIE: Not you, dear. The bag. I was looking for it. And when I asked where it was, you walked through the door.

FATHER MIKE: Oh.

(ALBERT *opens the bag and finds the compass.* LESLIE *sets it on the table and continues talking to* KATHRYN.)

LESLIE: The spiritual realm is not some distant place. It's all around us. All the time. But offset. So we start with physical north— (*She reads the compass, then points.*) —which is that way—

(ALBERT *motions to* JONATHAN *and they turn the table until the arrow on top marked "NORTH" is aimed in that direction.*)

LESLIE: --and then I'll use my psychic energy to find spiritual north and realign the space. That will open the door so the dead can see us and we can see them.

(LESLIE *puts the compass away and* ALBERT *walks around the room, double-checking the blackout drapes that have been hung on the windows and doors.*)

(KATHRYN *examines the table more closely.*)

KATHRYN: What are these other markings?

LESLIE: Sigils. Symbols with magical power.

JONATHAN: But they're mostly words.

ALBERT: Words are sigils, too.

(JONATHAN *lifts his eyebrows.*)

JONATHAN: What are you talking about? Words are just words.

LESLIE: No, Mr Vask. Think about it. Words are not at all the things they represent. And yet they contain those things. All the power of a lion, say, is contained within the word "lion", isn't it?

ALBERT: Which is why those in the middle ages believed speaking the devil's name was enough to summon him.

(KATHRYN *is still looking at the table.*)

KATHRYN: Is that what these are? Names? Raphael. Uriel. Gabriel. Michael.

FATHER MIKE: Those are the archangels.

LESLIE: That's right. And each one is aligned with particular forces. And each aspect of the table contains those forces. Four directions. Four elements. Four seasons. Four times of day. Four phases of the moon.

JONATHAN: Then why does it have five sides?

LESLIE: The five senses, of course. The center is the sixth sense. Our ability to sense beyond our senses, once we've opened the door.

FATHER MIKE: Sounds like alchemy.

LESLIE: You're right. Most people think alchemy was just about turning lead into gold. But it was much more spiritual than that.

(LESLIE *begins unpacking a series of items from the boxes: a triangular candle-holder similar to a pool table rack; three virgin 13-inch white candles; a nine-inch wide glass bowl; a jar of water; an 11-inch gold plate; and a seven-inch tall U-shaped iron rod mounted on an eight-inch wide piece of copper.*)

(KATHRYN *watches with fascination as* LESLIE *goes to work, putting the candles in the holder, then setting the triangle in the center of the table. She puts the glass bowl in the middle of the triangle and fills it with water from the jar.*)

KATHRYN: Is that holy water?

LESLIE: It is.

FATHER MIKE: Where did it come from?

ALBERT: A priest friend of ours makes it for us. Can you gentlemen please help me with the chairs?

(ALBERT, FATHER MIKE *and* JONATHAN *begin moving the chairs into position, one on each of the five sides.*)

(LESLIE *puts the gold plate on top of the bowl and the U-shaped iron rod on top of that. The last item is a silver bell, which she takes out of a black velvet bag and hangs from a hook in the top center of the U-shaped rod.*)

LESLIE: And this is the spirit bell. When it rings, we'll know the door is opened.

(KATHRYN *smiles, but with hesitation.*)

KATHRYN: I…suddenly feel scared.

LESLIE: That's a perfectly natural reaction to what we're doing. But do your best to put it out of your mind. We don't want to draw any unfriendly visitors.

KATHRYN: What do you mean?

LESLIE: This table will be like a lighthouse. We can't restrict what spirits it might attract. We hope Timothy sees it, of course. And only Timothy would be ideal. But chances are, we'll have some others to deal with.

JONATHAN: Others?

ALBERT: People who've died and may be here in our neck of the woods.

LESLIE: And like people in the land of the living: there are good ones and there are bad ones.

ALBERT: The bad ones have an uncanny ability to sense fear. It's like meat on a barbecue to them. Some are very angry about being dead and so they like to disrupt things for the living when they get the chance.

(KATHRYN *shivers and hugs herself.*)

KATHRYN: I'm sorry, but I'm even more scared now. I don't know if I want to go through with this.

JONATHAN: Are you kidding me?

(FATHER MIKE *puts his hand on* JONATHAN'*s shoulder.*)

FATHER MIKE: Jonathan, please.

(JONATHAN *shakes it off and approaches* KATHRYN.)

JONATHAN: You can't be serious.

LESLIE: Mr Vask.

JONATHAN: All of this is for you.

KATHRYN: I know. It's just…

LESLIE: Mr. Vask, if you don't stop what you're doing right now, I'll call off the sitting myself.

JONATHAN: You can't do that. I've already paid you.

ALBERT: But we can. And we will. The sort of energy you're creating is incredibly dangerous.

JONATHAN: Oh, right. I suppose my anger is just more meat on that metaphorical barbecue of yours.

ALBERT: It is. So please calm yourself or we will give you your money back and we will leave.

(JONATHAN *steps away.*)

KATHRYN: I'm sorry.

LESLIE: You have nothing to apologize for.

(JONATHAN *snorts.*)

LESLIE: I'm glad you're telling me how you feel now so we can deal with it. I've seen a number of sittings go very badly because people weren't honest. Understand?

(KATHRYN *nods.*)

LESLIE: Let's try a different way of thinking about it, okay?

KATHRYN: Sure.

LESLIE: Imagine for a moment that you have a fear of flying.

JONATHAN: She doesn't have to imagine.

LESLIE: No?

KATHRYN: I'm afraid of any sort of heights.

LESLIE: And have you flown before?

KATHRYN: To Hawaii. And New York. We were even planning a trip to Venice. Timothy had read a book about it and his dream was to visit one day.

LESLIE: So you prioritized. You decided going to those places was more important than your fear of flying.

KATHRYN: I guess so.

LESLIE: And what's more important right now? Your fear, or the chance to talk to Timothy?

KATHRYN: Talking to Timothy, of course.

(JONATHAN *looks at* FATHER MIKE, *relieved.*)

LESLIE: Then there's your answer. And if it's any help, think of me like those airline pilots. I've done hundreds of sittings. Put your trust in me. Can you do that?

KATHRYN: I'll try.

LESLIE: We'll take it slowly. If you feel you can't continue, tell me and we'll decide what's best as we go along. Okay?

(KATHRYN nods. LESLIE turns to the others.)

LESLIE: I'll sit facing north. Albert will take the chair to my right.

KATHRYN: Where do you want me?

LESLIE: On my left. Then your husband to your left and Father Mike next to Albert.

ALBERT: Mr Vask, before you take your seat, can you please turn off all the lights?

(As JONATHAN goes around the room switching off the lamps, ALBERT turns on the rack of lights between the cameras. They have red gels, which makes the space look like a photographer's darkroom.)

(ALBERT turns the cameras on, then brings a cord from one of the machines and wraps it around LESLIE's chest. Another cable is attached to a band which he places around the wrist of her right hand.)

JONATHAN: What's all that for?

ALBERT: The university. Records her heart rate, breathing, temperature. So they can track the changes her body goes through during the phases of the sitting. *(He returns to the lights.)* As soon as everyone is settled, we'll make sure the blackout drapes are working properly.

(They take their seats.)

ALBERT: All right. I'm going to switch these lights off now for about thirty seconds to make sure we have total darkness.

(ALBERT *turns the lights off.*)

ALBERT: Anyone see anything?

FATHER MIKE: I can't.

LESLIE: That's enough.

(ALBERT *switches the lights back on, then sits down.*)

LESLIE: Don't forget the rules we talked about. Both feet flat on the floor at all times. Do not speak unless spoken to. Once we have formed a circle, either by holding hands or touching our fingers together, it is absolutely critical that you do not break it for any reason other than my telling you it is okay to do so. The energy formed by our connection is what will protect from unfriendly visitors, should any show up. They will try to break our circle so they can get inside of it and use our energy against us. Do not allow that to happen.

(JONATHAN *trades a look with* FATHER MIKE.)

LESLIE: During the alignment process, you will see the lights get dimmer and brighter. Don't worry. That's a sign that it's working.

ALBERT: Are there any other questions before we begin?

(FATHER MIKE, JONATHAN, *and* KATHRYN *trade glances but say nothing.*)

ALBERT: Very well.

(LESLIE *takes out a small tuning fork. She strikes it against the palm of her hand, then holds the stalk on the gold plate that covers the bowl. The tone resonates loudly, but fades quickly. She repeats this process two more times, then puts the fork aside.*)

LESLIE: Everyone place your hands on the table inside the outlines. Make sure your thumbs are touching each other and your pinky fingers are touching those of the person next to you on both sides.

(After they comply, they are sitting straight-backed, feet on the floor, hands flat on the table, fingers touching all the way around.)

(LESLIE takes a deep breath and exhales. She closes her eyes and tips her head forward.)

(A low noise begins filling the room. It sounds mechanical at first, like the hum of a machine. But then it starts changing pitch and wavering.)

(The lights respond to the sound. They brighten as the pitch gets higher and dim as the pitch lowers.)

(ALBERT keeps his gaze fixed on LESLIE. The others trade nervous glances.)

(LESLIE lifts her head, revealing that her mouth is open. The sound is coming from her.)

(KATHRYN's eyes widen as the pitch climbs higher and the lights brighten again.)

(The pitch keeps going up and the lights get brighter—so much brighter that KATHRYN and the others need to squint.)

(Suddenly, LESLIE shuts her mouth and the lights go out completely, plunging the space into pitch black.)

(Silence.)

(The bell rings and KATHRYN screams.)

(The lights snap back on to reveal that Kathryn has broken the circle and is hugging JONATHAN.)

JONATHAN: It's okay. Sh-sh. Deep breaths now. In. Out. In. Out.

(KATHRYN complies and soon begins to calm down.)

JONATHAN: Okay?

(KATHRYN *nods and faces* LESLIE.)

KATHRYN: I broke the circle. I'm sorry.

LESLIE: It's okay. Lucky for us, we were in a safe spot.

JONATHAN: You don't scream the way she just did when you're safe.

KATHRYN: It wasn't like that.

JONATHAN: What do you mean?

KATHRYN: Didn't you feel it? It was like we were falling.

LESLIE: That's right.

JONATHAN: I didn't feel anything.

ALBERT: Not everyone is as sensitive to it as your wife obviously is.

KATHRYN: It happened when the bell rang.

LESLIE: That's right. We've realigned. Now we're oriented to spiritual north. The door is open.

(LESLIE *takes the bell off the hook on the U-shaped iron rod and puts it back into the black velvet bag. She takes the rod off the gold plate and gets out of her chair to put it away in the box on the floor. When she returns to the table, she has Timothy's Rubik's Cube.*)

(KATHRYN'*s breath catches in her throat.*)

(LESLIE *puts the Rubik's Cube in the center of the gold plate that covers the bowl of holy water.*)

KATHRYN: What now?

LESLIE: We'll close the circle again in a moment and then start trying to contact Timothy.

(KATHRYN *grabs* JONATHAN'*s hand and holds it tightly.*)

LESLIE: Please remember also the rule about materializations. If there are any—

KATHRYN: Don't touch them.

LESLIE: Right. No matter how strongly you want to. Do not.

(KATHRYN *nods.*)

JONATHAN: You're shaking like it's thirty degrees in here. Are you sure you're okay?

KATHRYN: I just can't believe this is finally happening.

JONATHAN: Maybe we should take a break. Get you a cup of tea or something.

LESLIE: We can't stop now.

KATHRYN: I don't want to anyway.

LESLIE: Good. The less time we spend aligned like this, the better.

ALBERT: Lights out?

(LESLIE *nods.* ALBERT *gets up from his chair and shuts off the rack of red lights. At the same moment, she strikes a long wooden match and uses it to light the three candles.*)

LESLIE: We'll hold hands this time. That will make the circle stronger.

(*Everyone takes the hand of the person next to them on both sides.*)

LESLIE: Ready?

(KATHRYN *nods.* LESLIE *closes her eyes.*)

(JONATHAN *looks at* FATHER MIKE *as if he can't quite believe what he's gotten himself into.*)

LESLIE: A terrible death has been suffered in this house. The death of a child. The death no parent expects to experience. Especially the kind of death that took Timothy Vask from his mother and father, here with us now. This death has become a heavy weight for them. This death has become a thick curtain of darkness on their lives. Lives that want to move on but cannot because of unresolved questions around this unexpected death. To those spirits who can hear me, please know that we do not like this heavy darkness. We come in peace. And though this death was violent, we do not intend violence, nor do we seek it. We are here for one purpose only: to find Timothy Vask so that his mother and father may ask him the questions they need to get the answers that will lead to resolution. To the lifting of this weight and the banishment of this darkness. *(She listens for a moment.)* Is there someone who can hear me? Is there someone who knows the one we seek? Is there someone who can help us find him? If so, use me now that we may accomplish these goals. Let my body become your body. Let my eyes and ears be yours. Let my mouth speak for you. *(She sits rock still for several seconds, then turns her head, as if looking over her left shoulder, even though her eyes remain closed.)* I see you. Don't be afraid. I spoke the truth when I said we don't want to hurt or be hurt.

(JONATHAN and KATHRYN look over their right shoulders, then face each other.)

LESLIE: Come closer so I can get a better look. *(Eyes still closed, she now moves her head, as if tracking a child approaching the table and walking around the group behind their chairs.)* It's okay. You can see there's nothing to fear here.

(ALBERT keeps his gaze fixed on LESLIE. FATHER MIKE, JONATHAN, and KATHRYN move their heads in tandem with LESLIE.)

LESLIE: That's right. Come into me. *(She is now "looking" over her right shoulder, as if the child is standing behind her.)* Come all the way in. *(She slowly turns her face toward the ceiling and sucks in a deep breath. As she exhales, she tips her head down, eyes still closed. Her face softens and takes on an expression of sadness.)*

ALBERT: Are you still here, Leslie?

(When LESLIE *speaks, her voice is like a child's.)*

LESLIE: *(As Rebecca)* Yes. She's here. But she's letting me talk to you. That's okay, right?

ALBERT: Of course it is. Who are you?

LESLIE: *(As Rebecca)* My name's Rebecca. I like to be called Becky, but Daddy doesn't want me to tell people that.

ALBERT: Would you like us to call you Becky?

LESLIE: *(As Rebecca)* Yes, please.

ALBERT: Okay, Becky. How old are you?

LESLIE: *(As Rebecca)* I don't know anymore. It's been ever so long since I had a birthday.

ALBERT: What was the last one you remember?

LESLIE: *(As Rebecca)* My eighth.

ALBERT: And where was it?

LESLIE: *(As Rebecca)* Here, silly. In my house.

ALBERT: This is your house?

LESLIE: *(As Rebecca)* That's what Daddy says. He says the others don't belong.

ALBERT: Do you mean Mr And Mrs Vask?

LESLIE: *(As Rebecca)* Not just them. Daddy's always glad when the people leave. That's why he's so mad now.

ALBERT: Because they won't leave?

LESLIE: *(As Rebecca)* Because of Timothy.

*(*KATHRYN*'s breath catches in her throat. She wants to say something, but* ALBERT *lifts his hand to stop her.)*

ALBERT: You know Timothy?

LESLIE: *(As Rebecca)* He's my friend. My only friend.

ALBERT: Is he there with you now?

LESLIE: *(As Rebecca)* No. He can't be.

ALBERT: Why not?

LESLIE: *(As Rebecca)* Because Daddy doesn't like him. He doesn't want us to play together, so we have to keep it a secret. We have lots of secrets.

ALBERT: But do you know where he is?

LESLIE: *(As Rebecca)* Sure. In our hiding place. That's one of our secrets. I showed it to him. It's the one I use when I'm hiding from daddy.

ALBERT: Can you go and get him for us?

LESLIE: *(As Rebecca)* I don't know.

ALBERT: Please. It's very important. His mommy and daddy want to talk to him.

LESLIE: *(As Rebecca)* But if my daddy finds out, we'll be in terrible trouble. Both of us. Daddy will hurt us.

(KATHRYN's eyes widen with worry and anguish.)

ALBERT: Is your Daddy there now?

LESLIE: *(As Rebecca)* Somewhere. He likes to hide, too. So he can watch.

ALBERT: Watch you?

LESLIE: *(As Rebecca)* Sometimes. But mostly whoever's in the house. He sees everything.

(Losing patience, JONATHAN leans forward.)

JONATHAN: Go get Timothy now.

ALBERT: Mr Vask. Please!

LESLIE: *(As Rebecca)* Who was that?

ALBERT: Timothy's father.

LESLIE: *(As Rebecca)* Oh. Hello.

*(*JONATHAN *looks at* ALBERT. ALBERT *gestures: "Go ahead".)*

JONATHAN: Hello. I really want to talk to Timothy. So can you be a good girl and run along to get him for me?

LESLIE: *(As Rebecca)* I can try.

ALBERT: That's all we ask.

LESLIE: *(As Rebecca)* Okay. *(She droops forward like a puppet with cut strings. When she lifts her head this time, she blinks rapidly, as if waking from a deep sleep.)*

ALBERT: Everything okay?

*(*LESLIE *nods at* ALBERT, *then looks at the others.)*

LESLIE: Maintain the circle, please.

KATHRYN: Can I ask a question?

LESLIE: Yes, but quickly.

KATHRYN: What did she mean about her father hurting her? How can he?

LESLIE: Obviously, it's not physical. From what I understand, it's more to do with energy. Sort of like how you feel when someone is angry with you. They don't need to touch you to cause harm.

KATHRYN: And he could hurt Timothy in the same way?

LESLIE: Sounds like it.

KATHRYN: But that has to stop. How can I stop it?

LESLIE: Calm down, first of all. This is not something I expected. I need time to figure out exactly what's happening. Most likely, these spirits are attached to this place because of how they died. They may be holding Timothy. Hopefully, what we're doing tonight will—

(LESLIE *stops talking when a thunderous boom shakes the house.*)

(KATHRYN *screams.*)

LESLIE: Do not break the circle.

(*The lamps flicker on and off.*)

(*Silence*)

(*And then* LESLIE's *head snaps violently forward and back.*)

(*She sucks in a breath that sounds like concrete blocks scraping against each other and leans over, her nose barely an inch from the table top.*)

(*Her breathing changes. It is deep and raspy, like someone with emphysema.*)

(*She lifts her head again, eyes closed. Her face is pinched and angry.*)

ALBERT: Becky?

(*When* LESLIE *speaks now, her voice is that of an old man.*)

LESLIE: (*As Jack*) No. And her name is Rebecca.

ALBERT: Are you her father?

LESLIE: (*As Jack*) Yes. And I want you all to leave here now. You're trespassing.

ALBERT: No we're not. The owners invited us.

LESLIE: (*As Jack*) This house doesn't belong to them. It belongs to me. I built it. So leave. All of you. Never come back.

ALBERT: Not until we talk to Timothy.

LESLIE: (*As Jack*) Only if you tell him to stay away from my daughter.

KATHRYN: We can do that. But you have to stop hurting him.

LESLIE: *(As Jack)* Or what, hmm?

KATHRYN: It wasn't a threat. I was just asking.

LESLIE: *(As Jack)* About all you can do, isn't it? A little bitty pretty one like you. So delicate. So fragile. So broken.

(Tears run down KATHRYN's cheeks. She lifts JONATHAN's hand with hers so she can wipe them away without breaking the circle.)

JONATHAN: All right, that's enough. Leave her alone.

LESLIE: *(As Jack)* Says the Big Bad Husband. Why? Is it because you don't want her pain going to anyone but you?

JONATHAN: Okay. I'm serious. I've had enough of this. We need to get to Timothy.

LESLIE: *(As Jack)* Are you sure that's a good idea?

JONATHAN: That's why we're doing this.

LESLIE: *(As Jack)* But aren't you afraid of what he might say?

JONATHAN: What is this? What's going on? You didn't tell me any of this was going to happen.

(KATHRYN looks at JONATHAN, confused.)

KATHRYN: Who didn't tell you?

JONATHAN: Them. The Harmons.

KATHRYN: Yes, they did. They said we might have others to deal with.

(FATHER MIKE pulls JONATHAN's hand.)

FATHER MIKE: That's right, Jonathan. I think you should let them continue. We wouldn't want to stop now that we're so close. Would we?

(JONATHAN *grits his teeth.* LESLIE *laughs, deep and raspy, then moves her head back and forth, sniffing the air.*)

LESLIE: *(As Jack)* So sweet. That fear I smell.

JONATHAN: It's not fear. It's anger. And if anyone should be scared, it's you.

LESLIE: *(As Jack)* What should I be afraid of?

JONATHAN: What I'll do to you if you don't get this thing back on track.

LESLIE: *(As Jack)* In good time.

ALBERT: Can you get Timothy or not?

LESLIE: *(As Jack)* I can't. But Rebecca can. If I tell her it's okay.

ALBERT: Do that for us and we can help him leave here.

LESLIE: *(As Jack)* Sure about that?

ALBERT: Yes.

LESLIE: *(As Jack)* You don't think I want to move on? Me and Rebecca both?

ALBERT: It didn't sound like it.

LESLIE: *(As Jack)* Because I've accepted the fact that we can't.

ALBERT: Why not?

LESLIE: *(As Jack)* Because of how we got here. Same as Timothy.

ALBERT: You died in an accident?

LESLIE: *(As Jack)* That's what the papers said. But they didn't know the truth. My wife and her new husband made sure of that.

ALBERT: Are you saying you were murdered?

LESLIE: *(As Jack)* Poisoned by them to take my house.

ALBERT: And you can't move on because you were murdered?

LESLIE: *(As Jack)* Give that man a cigar.

KATHRYN: But Timothy died in an accident.

LESLIE: *(As Jack)* Same as me.

JONATHAN: Mr Harmon, what purpose is this serving?

(LESLIE turns her head and looks into the darkness behind FATHER MIKE.)

LESLIE: *(As Jack)* Here they are now.

KATHRYN: Timothy?

LESLIE: *(As Jack)* And Rebecca.

JONATHAN: Finally.

KATHRYN: Jonathan, please.

(JONATHAN glares at ALBERT.)

LESLIE: *(As Jack)* Come here, Timothy. It's okay. I won't hurt you. Not this time. Your mom wants to talk to you. And your dad is here, too. Isn't that nice?

(LESLIE droops. Her ragged breath changes, becoming shallow and rapid.)

(Her voice is a child's again, but a boy this time.)

LESLIE: *(As Timothy)* Mom?

(The dam breaks and waves of conflicting emotions wash across KATHRYN's face.)

KATHRYN: Oh, my God: Timothy! Baby. Mom's right here.

LESLIE: *(As Timothy)* I miss you.

KATHRYN: I miss you, too. And so does Dad.

JONATHAN: That's right, son. I do.

LESLIE: *(As Timothy)* No, you don't.

(The relief JONATHAN *was feeling is replaced by anger.)*

JONATHAN: What the hell?

KATHRYN: Jonathan, stop.

JONATHAN: No. They need to stop.

KATHRYN: Not now!

LESLIE: *(As Timothy)* I'm sorry, Mom.

KATHRYN: It's okay, honey. I'm sorry. That's why I'm here. I wanted to tell you how sorry I am and I wanted to know you understand that how you died was a terrible accident and that you don't blame me.

LESLIE: *(As Timothy)* I don't.

KATHRYN: You don't?

LESLIE: *(As Timothy)* No. It's not your fault.

*(*FATHER MIKE *looks at* JONATHAN. JONATHAN *seems relieved again.)*

LESLIE: *(As Timothy)* It's Dad's.

KATHRYN: No, honey. It's not his fault either.

LESLIE: *(As Timothy)* Yes it is. He made me fall down the stairs.

KATHRYN: No, he didn't.

LESLIE: *(As Timothy)* Yes, he did. He came home without Mrs Willingham knowing. He made me have a seizure at the top of the stairs so I would fall down and then he waited until he was sure I was dead before he sneaked out.

*(*KATHRYN *stares, dumbfounded.)*

JONATHAN: Is this your idea of a joke?

LESLIE: *(As Timothy)* No, Dad. It's your idea of a joke. You and Father Mike. Tell her.

JONATHAN: What the fuck are you doing?

KATHRYN: I don't understand. What's going on?

JONATHAN: Yeah, Albert. What's going on?

(ALBERT has an expression of honest panic.)

ALBERT: I assure you, Mr Vask, I don't know.

JONATHAN: What do you mean you don't know?

(FATHER MIKE gasps.)

FATHER MIKE: Oh, my God.

JONATHAN: What?

FATHER MIKE: It's for real.

JONATHAN: Oh, please. Don't give me that bullshit.

KATHRYN: Of course it's for real. Isn't it?

LESLIE: *(As Timothy)* Yes, it is.

(JONATHAN pulls his hands away from Kathryn and FATHER MIKE.)

JONATHAN: Cut the shit. I've had it.

KATHRYN: Don't break the circle!

(KATHRYN tries to grab JONATHAN's hand. He pushes it away.)

JONATHAN: It's bullshit, Kathryn. All of it. This was Father Mike's idea.

(LESLIE starts laughing. But it's quiet and creepy.)

JONATHAN: Will you please shut your wife up?

LESLIE: *(As Timothy)* I'm not his wife.

JONATHAN: Oh, my God. I need a drink.

(KATHRYN grabs JONATHAN.)

KATHRYN: No. Tell me what is happening.

JONATHAN: This whole thing was a put on. We wanted you to think we were talking to Timothy so that he could say he forgives you and you could finally get over it.

LESLIE: *(As Timothy)* Keep going.

(JONATHAN *looks at* LESLIE, *then at* ALBERT.*)*

JONATHAN: Can you please stop? It's over.

LESLIE: *(As Timothy)* Not until you tell her the truth.

JONATHAN: I just did.

LESLIE: *(As Timothy)* About me, Dad. About what you did to me.

(JONATHAN *sees how everyone is staring.)*

JONATHAN: What are you looking at me like that for?

KATHRYN: What is he talking about?

JONATHAN: It's not Timothy. Okay? They're actors. And they can quit acting now because it's over.

LESLIE: *(As Timothy)* Tell them how you used the strobe light.

(JONATHAN*'s eyes snap from face to face.)*

JONATHAN: It's ridiculous.

LESLIE: *(As Timothy)* Tell them how you pretended to be at that engineering conference but you really came here.

KATHRYN: That was the day it happened. I remember that.

JONATHAN: Kathryn, please.

LESLIE: *(As Timothy)* You unbalanced the washing machine so Mrs Willingham would go in the basement.

JONATHAN: This is insane.

LESLIE: *(As Timothy)* And then you brought my Rubik's Cube to me and flashed that light in my eyes.

(JONATHAN*'s expression changes.)*

JONATHAN: But this is impossible. You're not really my son. You can't be.

LESLIE: *(As Timothy)* That's what you always told yourself, wasn't it? You could never be the father of something like me.

JONATHAN: I couldn't.

LESLIE: *(As Timothy)* But you are.

(KATHRYN stares at JONATHAN.)

KATHRYN: Did you really think that?

(JONATHAN can't answer.)

LESLIE: *(As Timothy)* Look at his face.

(KATHRYN stares at JONATHAN.)

KATHRYN: Is it true?

LESLIE: *(As Timothy)* Tell her, Dad.

JONATHAN: Stop pretending to be my son.

LESLIE: *(As Timothy)* I'm not pretending.

KATHRYN: It is true.

JONATHAN: What? No.

KATHRYN: Is that why you did it? Because you didn't think he was yours?

JONATHAN: No.

KATHRYN: Why, then?

LESLIE: *(As Timothy)* For the money.

JONATHAN: Not like that.

KATHRYN: So you did do it.

(JONATHAN slams his fists on the table.)

JONATHAN: For you. For us. I wanted us to be free. Of all the pain he caused. That's all. It was better for him, too. Don't you see that?

(ALBERT *turns the lights on.*)

(*When the lights go on this time, they are white instead of red.*)

(KATHRYN *turns away.* JONATHAN *sees* ALBERT *pointing a revolver at him.*)

ALBERT: Would you repeat that for the cameras, please?

(JONATHAN *stares at him, more dumbfounded than ever.*)

(LESLIE *opens her eyes.*)

JONATHAN: What is this? Kathryn?

(*But* KATHRYN *is broken. Tears stream across her cheeks.*)

KATHRYN: I didn't want to believe it. But I knew somehow all the same.

JONATHAN: What's going on?

(FATHER MIKE *stands up. He's holding handcuffs.*)

FATHER MIKE: Put your hands behind your back, Jonathan.

(*When* JONATHAN *doesn't comply,* ALBERT *cocks the revolver.*)

ALBERT: Please, Mr Vask. Do as he says.

(FATHER MIKE *takes one of* JONATHAN's *wrists in his hand and pulls it behind the chair.*)

(*Reluctantly,* JONATHAN *gives him the other hand and* FATHER MIKE *ratchets the cuffs in place.*)

(JONATHAN *looks around the room, still trying to figure out what has just happened.*)

JONATHAN: How did you know?

(LESLIE *puts her arms around* KATHRYN.)

KATHRYN: Timothy told me.

(JONATHAN *sags.*)

JONATHAN: Please. Don't.

FATHER MIKE: Back to not believing again already?

JONATHAN: You don't think I really thought any of that was for real.

ALBERT: Looked like it to me. *(He motions to the cameras over his shoulder.)* Should we play it back for you?

(JONATHAN sneers.)

KATHRYN: It's true. I really was having those nightmares. But then Timothy started talking to me and I could tell there was something different about it. When he told me what you had done, I didn't know what to do. I told Doctor Tanner and he said it was just my imagination. That was when I quit seeing him.

FATHER MIKE: Then she came to see me. About a month before she told you she wanted to. I told her we should go to the police.

KATHRYN: But I said that would be pointless.

ALBERT: And she was right.

JONATHAN: You mean...?

(ALBERT reaches into his jacket and takes out a wallet. He opens it to show a police badge.)

ALBERT: They didn't know it at the time, but the insurance investigator who finally approved the settlement told me there was no way he could prove it wasn't an accident. But he had a nagging feeling that maybe I should take a closer look.

FATHER MIKE: By that time, Kathryn had checked some of what Timothy had said in her dreams.

KATHRYN: And it was all true.

ALBERT: They were planning on doing this thing with Leslie by herself. I asked if I could help.

JONATHAN: You've got nothing, then.

ALBERT: We've got your confession.

JONATHAN: But I can take that back. I can say I was scared. You coerced me.

ALBERT: You could try. But it's enough for us to get a warrant for the security cameras at the convention center. Are you sure that none of them will show you leaving roughly thirty minutes before Mrs. Willingham called 9-1-1?

(JONATHAN *looks at* KATHRYN.)

JONATHAN: We could have been so happy. If you hadn't felt guilty.

KATHRYN: I don't know whether to hate you or feel sorry for you.

JONATHAN: Feel sorry for yourself. They'll take the money away now.

KATHRYN: I don't care about that.

JONATHAN: You should. Without me, you'll have nothing.

(KATHRYN *wipes her eyes in silence.* JONATHAN *turns his head toward the stairs and smirks.*)

JONATHAN: Enough already, okay?

ALBERT: Enough what?

JONATHAN: With this spirit magic bullshit. I get it. You're good. You fooled me but it's over now. You got what you wanted.

FATHER MIKE: What are you talking about?

(JONATHAN *motions toward the stairs with his chin.*)

JONATHAN: Him. Is he supposed to be Timothy? It doesn't even look like him.

(*Everyone faces the stairs, but they are empty.*)

FATHER MIKE: Who?

JONATHAN: It's not funny anymore.

FATHER MIKE: I'm not trying to be funny.

JONATHAN: The kid on the stairs.

ALBERT: There's no one on the stairs, Mr Vask.

JONATHAN: Let me up and I'll prove it.

(JONATHAN *tries to stand, but can't because of how he's handcuffed.*)

ALBERT: Stay in your chair, please.

JONATHAN: Then make him stop. Tell him to stay away from me.

ALBERT: There's nobody else here.

JONATHAN: Stop lying to me.

(JONATHAN *starts thrashing on the chair. He's looking at the space next to him as if he's tracking a child.*)

JONATHAN: Get him away from me. *(He snaps his head the other way.)* Stop it.

(JONATHAN *starts kicking violently. He connects with one of* FATHER MIKE's *shins and the priest stumbles backwards.*)

(KATHRYN *and* LESLIE *stand and back away.*)

JONATHAN: Stop! Get away from me!

(JONATHAN *throws himself to one side and the chair tips. He hits the floor hard and starts trying to crawl away.*)

(*But then he freezes, as if something is holding him in place. He gasps and his mouth opens and closes as his eyes roll back in his head.*)

LESLIE: What's happening?

FATHER MIKE: I think he's having a heart attack.

ALBERT: Someone call 9-1-1.

JONATHAN: Noooo!

(JONATHAN *lets out a horrible gasp and his body shakes before going totally limp.*)

(Everyone stares for several seconds until ALBERT *crouches next to him and checks his pulse.)*

ALBERT: He's dead.

*(*KATHRYN *turns her face into* LESLIE*'s shoulder.* FATHER MIKE *covers his mouth with one hand.)*

*(*ALBERT *stands, then holsters his gun.)*

(Black out)

Scene 2

(Weeks later. Grey sunlight through the opaque curtains. The whole place is empty now except for a pair of suitcases in the middle of the room.)

(The doorbell rings and KATHRYN *comes down the stairs with her purse over one shoulder and a jacket over her arm. She opens the front door and* FATHER MIKE *enters. He's wearing a wet trench coat over his clerical clothing.)*

KATHRYN: Still raining?

FATHER MIKE: Just a bit. How are you?

KATHRYN: Better.

FATHER MIKE: Good. I keep forgetting to ask: did that buyer I told you about ever get in touch?

KATHRYN: I thought you knew. We're in escrow now. We should close in two weeks. Right after I get back.

FATHER MIKE: Excellent. So that's it, then.

KATHRYN: Almost. I'm still dealing with the insurance company. Jonathan was right. His confession made Timothy's policy void.

FATHER MIKE: They took the money back?

KATHRYN: No. Jonathan's policy was bigger, so they've decided to just pay the difference.

FATHER MIKE: Jonathan's policy?

KATHRYN: Because of his heart attack.

(FATHER MIKE's *eyes widen.*)

FATHER MIKE: Oh, my. It's almost as if…

KATHRYN: I don't think there's any almost about it. Do you?

FATHER MIKE: No. I guess you're right about that.

(KATHRYN *checks her watch.*)

KATHRYN: I hate to hurry this along, but I've got a plane to catch.

FATHER MIKE: Oh, right. Sorry. Are you flying straight to Venice?

KATHRYN: I have to change planes in Rome.

FATHER MIKE: That's a long flight. Will you be okay?

KATHRYN: It's strange, you know. I don't feel scared anymore.

(FATHER MIKE *nods.*)

KATHRYN: So?

(FATHER MIKE *reaches into his jacket pocket and takes out Timothy's Rubik's Cube.*)

FATHER MIKE: Here it is.

(FATHER MIKE *hands it to* KATHRYN *and she puts it into her purse.*)

FATHER MIKE: Leslie wanted me to be sure you knew how sorry she was for taking so long to get it back to you.

(KATHRYN *puts on her jacket.*)

KATHRYN: It's all right. Tell her I had lots of other things on my mind.

(*A horn honks O S.*)

FATHER MIKE: That'll be your ride. Help you carry those?

(KATHRYN *nods.* FATHER MIKE *picks up her suitcases and goes out the front door.*)

(*She follows him for a few steps, then stops. She turns around, scanning the space, a forlorn expression on her face.*)

(*The horn honks O S again and* KATHRYN *hurries out, closing the front door behind her with a decisive click.*)

(*From somewhere, a breeze moves the curtains.*)

(*Black out*)

END OF PLAY